AI MASTERY SOLUTIONS

ChatGPT: A Beginner's Guide to Using OpenAI's Language Model

Contents

1

Chapter 1: Introduction to ChatGPT

Welcome to the world of ChatGPT, the powerful language model that can generate human-like text and perform a wide range of language-related tasks. In this chapter, we'll be giving you a fun and informative guide on how to start using ChatGPT.

First things first, in order to start using ChatGPT, you'll need to create a user account on the OpenAI website. Don't worry, it's a quick and easy process! Here's what you need to do:

1. Go to **https://openai.com** and click on the "Sign Up" button.
2. Fill in the required fields, including your name, email address, and password.
3. Click on the "Sign Up" button again and voila! You now have a user account on the OpenAI website.

Now that you have an account, it's time to log in and start using ChatGPT. Here's how:

1. Go to **https://openai.com** and click on the "Log In" button.
2. Enter your email address and password.
3. Click on the "Log In" button and you'll be taken to the OpenAI dashboard.

Now that you're logged in, you'll have access to a variety of tools, including the ability to use ChatGPT. To use ChatGPT, simply click on the "GPT-3 Playground" button on the dashboard. This will take you to the GPT-3 Playground, where you can input a prompt and generate text using ChatGPT.

You can also customize your output by adjusting the length of the generated text, the model's temperature and top_p values. You can also use the prompt to perform other language-related tasks like summarization, sentiment analysis, and language translation.

One fun way of using ChatGPT is by using it to complete text passages, write short stories, or even write poetry. With the right input and a bit of creativity, you can get amazing results from ChatGPT.

It's important to remember that ChatGPT is a powerful tool, but it has its limitations, including potential biases in the generated text. It's always good to fine-tune the model with a diverse dataset to improve its performance and reduce bias.

Capabilities

ChatGPT has a wide range of capabilities, including:

- Language generation: ChatGPT can generate text that is similar to human-written text in terms of grammar, style, and content. It can also generate text in a specific style or tone, depending on the input provided.
- Language understanding: ChatGPT has a good understanding of the meaning of text, which allows it to generate text that is coherent and relevant to the given prompt.
- Language translation: ChatGPT can also perform language translation by providing the input in one language and the desired output in another language.
- Text summarization: ChatGPT can summarize text by extracting the most important information from it.
- Sentiment analysis: ChatGPT can also analyze the sentiment of a given text and predict whether it is positive, negative or neutral.

Limitations

Despite its many capabilities, ChatGPT also has some limitations. These include:

- Bias: ChatGPT is trained on a large dataset of text data, which may contain biases. As a result, the model's output may also be biased. To mitigate this, it's important to fine-tune the model on a diverse dataset.
- Lack of context: ChatGPT can generate text that is coherent and relevant to the given prompt, but it may lack context. For example, if given a prompt like "What is the capital of France?", it will return "Paris" but it can't provide more context than that.
-
- Repetition: As ChatGPT is trained on a large dataset, it may repeat the same information. To mitigate this, you can adjust the model's temperature and top_p values to avoid repeating the same information.

Implementation

Implementing ChatGPT is relatively straightforward and can be done in a few steps:

1. Download and install the necessary software: This includes installing the OpenAI Python library and obtaining an API key from OpenAI.
2. Provide input to ChatGPT: This can be done by specifying a prompt and any additional parameters, such as the length of the output or the desired output style.
3. Interpreting the output: The output generated by ChatGPT will be in the form of text, which can be further processed or used in an application.
4. Fine-tune the model: To better suit specific use cases, you can fine-tune the model on a smaller dataset. This will improve the model's performance and reduce bias.

In conclusion, ChatGPT is a powerful language model that can generate human-like text and perform a wide range of language-related tasks. However, it is important to be aware of its limitations and fine-tune the model as needed. With the right input and fine-tuning, ChatGPT can be a useful tool for various natural language processing tasks. Remember to have fun and be creative with the possibilities that ChatGPT offers.

2

Chapter 2: Setting up ChatGPT

Welcome back to our guide on using ChatGPT! In this chapter, we'll be diving into the fun and easy process of setting up ChatGPT on your device.

Before we begin, it's important to note that in order to use ChatGPT, you'll need to have an API key from OpenAI. If you haven't already, make sure to sign up for an account on the OpenAI website and obtain an API key.

Step 1: Install the OpenAI Python Library

The first step in setting up ChatGPT is to install the OpenAI Python library. This library allows you to easily interact with the OpenAI API and use ChatGPT in your Python projects.

To install the library, simply open a terminal and type in the following command:

```
pip install openai
```

Step 2: Set up the API Key

Once the library is installed, you'll need to set up your API key. This can be done by setting the **openai** environment variable to your API key.

You can set the environment variable by adding the following line to your **.bashrc** or **.bash_profile** file:

```
export OPENAI_API_KEY="your_api_key"
```

Make sure to replace **"your_api_key"** with your actual API key.

Step 3: Test the Setup

Now that you've set up the API key, it's a good idea to test the setup by running a simple test script. You can use the following script as an example:

```
import openai

openai.api_key = os.environ.get("OPENAI_API_KEY")

response = openai.Completion.create(
    engine="text-davinci-002",
    prompt='What is the capital of France?'
)

print(response["choices"][0]["text"])
```

This script will use the OpenAI API to generate a response to the prompt "What is the capital of France?" and should return "Paris".

In addition to using the OpenAI library, you can also use ChatGPT via the web browser using the command prompt at **https://chat.openai.com/**. This is a simple way to access ChatGPT's capabilities without any additional setup.

To use ChatGPT via the web browser, simply go to **https://chat.openai.com/** and log in with your OpenAI account. Once logged in, you'll be able to input a prompt and generate text in real-time.

You can also customize your output by adjusting the length of the generated text, the model's temperature and top_p values. You can also use the prompt to perform other language-related tasks like summarization, sentiment analysis, and language translation.

It's important to note that when using the web browser, you won't have access to the full range of capabilities that the OpenAI library offers. However, it's a great option for quick and easy access to ChatGPT's capabilities.

In summary, you can use ChatGPT by installing the OpenAI library and setting up the API key, or by using the web browser command prompt at

https://chat.openai.com/. Both options offer different levels of customization and access to ChatGPT's capabilities.

With the setup done, you're ready to start generating text and exploring the world of natural language processing with ChatGPT. Have fun!

3

Chapter 3: Basic Input and Output

Welcome to the third chapter of our guide on using ChatGPT! In this chapter, we'll be taking a closer look at the basics of inputting prompts and understanding the output generated by ChatGPT.

Inputting Prompts

The first step in using ChatGPT is to input a prompt. A prompt is a piece of text that the model uses as a starting point to generate text. The prompt can be anything from a single word to a full sentence or even a full story.

When inputting a prompt, it's important to keep in mind that the more specific and detailed the prompt is, the more specific and detailed the output will be. For example, if you input the prompt "Write a story about a robot that saves the world," ChatGPT will generate a story about a robot saving the world. If you input the prompt "Write a story," ChatGPT will generate a generic story.

Here are a few examples of prompts and the resulting output:

Prompt: "What is the capital of France?" Output: "Paris"

Prompt: "Tell me a joke" Output: "Why did the tomato turn red? Because it saw the salad dressing!"

Prompt: "Write a short story about a robot" Output: "Once upon a time, there was a robot named Max. Max was different from other robots, he had feelings and emotions. He was created to help people and make their lives easier, but he didn't just want to do that, he wanted to understand and experience life for himself. One day, Max decided to leave the factory and explore the world. He saw many things, met many people, and had many adventures. In the end, Max realized that the most important thing in life is to be true to oneself and to help others. And so, he returned to the factory, but this time, he was not the same robot that had left. He was better, he was more human."

Understanding Output

Once you've input a prompt, ChatGPT will generate text based on the prompt. The output can be in the form of a single word, a phrase, a sentence, or even a full story.

It's important to keep in mind that the output generated by ChatGPT may not always be perfect. The model is trained on a large dataset of text data, which may contain biases. As a result, the model's output may also be biased. To mitigate this, it's important to fine-tune the model on a diverse dataset.

In addition, ChatGPT's output may lack context, it can't provide more information than what is given in the prompt. For example, if you ask "What is the capital of France?" it will return "Paris" but it can't provide more context than that.

To get the most out of ChatGPT, it's important to experiment with different prompts and fine-tune the model as needed. With the right input and fine-tuning, ChatGPT can generate text that is similar to human-written text in terms of grammar, style, and content.

It's also important to pay attention to the temperature and top_p values when generating output. Temperature controls the randomness of the generated text, a higher temperature will result in more random and creative text, while a lower temperature will result in more conservative and repetitive text. top_p controls the proportion of the mass of the distribution that is used. A higher top_p value will result in the model being more conservative and only choosing from the most likely options, while a lower top_p value will allow the model to be more creative and explore less likely options.

Another thing to note is that GPT-3 has different models and you can use them depending on the task. For example, for text completion, you can use "text-davinci-002", for text generation "text-curie-001" and for language translation "text-babbage-001".

When reviewing the output, it's important to consider the context and intent of the prompt, as well as the potential biases and limitations of the model. With this understanding, you can use ChatGPT to generate text that is relevant, coherent, and useful.

In conclusion, inputting prompts and understanding the output generated by ChatGPT is an important step in using the model. By experimenting with different prompts and fine-tuning the model as needed, you can generate text that is similar to human-written text. Keep in mind the temperature, top_p and the model you are using to improve the output. Have fun and be creative with the possibilities that ChatGPT offers!

4

Chapter 4: Advanced Input and Output

Welcome back to our guide on using ChatGPT! In the previous chapter, we covered the basics of inputting prompts and understanding the output generated by the model. In this chapter, we'll be diving into some advanced techniques for inputting prompts and using the output in more advanced ways.

Prompt Control Tokens

Prompt control tokens are special tokens that can be added to a prompt to provide additional information to the model. These tokens can be used to control the type of output generated, the format of the output, and more.

For example, the "|" token can be used to specify where the model should continue generating text. For example, if you input the prompt "The robot was programmed to be able to speak in many languages. |" the model will continue generating text from the point after the "|" token.

Another example is the "!" token, this can be used to control the format of the output, for example, you can use "!p" to tell the model to generate a poem or "!s" to tell the model to generate a song.

Here are a few examples of how to use prompt control tokens:

Prompt: "The robot was programmed to be able to speak in many languages. |" Output: "and it was proud of its ability to communicate with people from all over the world. It was determined to learn even more languages and to help bridge the language barriers that existed between people."

Prompt: "Write a poem about the moon" Output: "The moon, a pale white light, Shines down on us at night. A beacon in the sky, Guiding us through the night.

It waxes and it wanes, Changing every day. But always it remains, A constant in our way."

Prompt: "Write a song about the ocean" Output: "Verse 1: The ocean, so vast and wide A never-ending tide It calls to me, a siren's song A place where I belong

Chorus: The ocean, my heart and soul A place where I can be whole It sings to me, a melody A symphony

Verse 2: The ocean, so dark and deep A place where secrets keep It whispers to me, a mystery A history

Chorus: The ocean, my heart and soul A place where I can be whole It sings to me, a melody A symphony

Outro: The ocean, my heart and soul It's where I feel whole."

Using Output in Applications

Once you have generated text using ChatGPT, you can use the output in various applications. For example, you can use the output to generate content for chatbots, virtual assistants, language translation and summarization, and more.

One example of an application is to use the output in a chatbot. You can use the output to generate responses to user queries.

Another example is to use the output to generate summaries of articles or news. You can use the output to generate a summary of the main ideas of the article.

In addition, you can use the output to generate subtitles for videos, or to generate captions for images.

It's important to note that when using the output in applications, it's important to fine-tune the model as needed, and to consider the potential biases and limitations of the model. With this understanding, you can use ChatGPT to generate text that is relevant, coherent, and useful in various applications.

Another example of an application is using the output in a virtual assistant. You can use the output to generate responses to user queries, such as answering questions, providing information, and performing tasks. For example, you can use ChatGPT to generate responses to user's questions about the weather, news, or sports.

Another example of an application is using the output to generate natural language translations. You can use the output to translate text from one language to another, such as translating a sentence from English to Spanish or French.

In addition, you can use the output to generate text that can be used in creative applications, such as writing poetry, composing music, or writing fiction.

It's also worth noting that OpenAI provide some pre-trained models for some specific tasks such as:

- DALL-E for image to text
- DALL-E 2 for text to image
- DALL-E3 for image manipulation
- Ada for text classification, question answering and more

By experimenting with different applications, you can discover new and exciting ways to use ChatGPT. The possibilities are endless, and with a little creativity, you can use the output generated by ChatGPT to create something truly unique.

In conclusion, advanced input techniques such as prompt control tokens, and using the output in various applications can help you to get the most out of ChatGPT. Remember to fine-tune the model as needed and be aware of its potential biases and limitations. Have fun and be creative with the possibilities that ChatGPT offers!

5

Chapter 5: Fine-Tuning ChatGPT

In this chapter, we will dive into the process of fine-tuning ChatGPT to improve the quality and relevance of its output. Fine-tuning is the process of training the model on a new dataset to adjust its parameters and improve its performance for a specific task or domain.

Fine-tuning can be done in two ways:

1. Transfer Learning: This method is used when you have a small dataset and you want to fine-tune the model on this dataset.
2. Full fine-tuning: This method is used when you have a large dataset and you want to fine-tune the model on this dataset.

Transfer Learning

Transfer learning is a technique where a pre-trained model is used as a starting point and then fine-tuned on a new dataset. This method is useful when you have a small dataset and you want to fine-tune the model to a specific task or domain.

The process of transfer learning involves first pre-training the model on a large dataset, and then fine-tuning it on a smaller dataset. This allows the model to learn the general patterns and features of the large dataset, while also learning the specific patterns and features of the smaller dataset.

To perform transfer learning with ChatGPT, you will need to use the OpenAI

API and the GPT-3 model. First, you will need to pre-train the model on a large dataset, such as the Common Crawl or Wikipedia dataset. Next, you will need to fine-tune the model on your smaller dataset.

Here's an example of how to fine-tune ChatGPT on a smaller dataset:

```
import openai

openai.api_key = os.environ.get("OPENAI_API_KEY")

model_engine = "text-davinci-002"

# Pre-training the model on a large dataset
response = openai.Model.create(
    model=model_engine,
    dataset="Common Crawl",
    prompt="Write a story about a robot that saves the world"
)

# Fine-tuning the model on a smaller dataset
response = openai.Model.create(
    model=model_engine,
    dataset="My Custom Dataset",
    prompt="Write a story about a robot that saves the world"
)
```

Full Fine-Tuning

Another method of fine-tuning is full fine-tuning, this method is used when you have a large dataset and you want to fine-tune the model on this dataset. This method is useful for tasks that require a large amount of data to be fine-tuned, such as language translation, text classification and more.

To perform full fine-tuning, you will need to use the OpenAI API and the GPT-3 model. First, you will need to provide the API with your dataset and the task you want the model to learn. Next, you will need to fine-tune the model on your dataset.

Here's an example of how to fine-tune ChatGPT on a large dataset:

```
import openai

openai.api_key = os.environ.get("OPENAI_API_KEY")

model_engine = "text-davinci-002"

#Fine-tuning the model on a large dataset
response = openai.Model.create(
model=model_engine,
dataset="My Large Dataset",
task="text-classification"
)


Using the fine-tuned model
response = openai.Completion.create(
model=response["id"],
prompt="Write a text classification on this article",
temperature=0.5
)
```

It's important to note that fine-tuning the model may take a long time and requires a significant amount of computational resources. It's also important to keep in mind that the quality and relevance of the output generated by the fine-tuned model will depend on the quality and relevance of the dataset used for fine-tuning.

In conclusion, fine-tuning is a powerful technique for improving the performance of ChatGPT. By fine-tuning the model on a specific task or domain, you can generate text that is more relevant and useful. Remember that the process of fine-tuning can be time-consuming and requires a significant amount of computational resources, but the results are worth it. Have fun and keep experimenting with different datasets and tasks!

6

Chapter 6: Using ChatGPT in Applications

In this chapter, we will explore how ChatGPT can be used in various applications. ChatGPT is a powerful language model that can be used to generate text for a wide range of applications, such as chatbots, virtual assistants, language translation, and more.

Chatbots

Chatbots are computer programs that can simulate conversation with human users. They can be used in a wide range of applications, such as customer service, e-commerce, and more. ChatGPT can be used to generate text for chatbots, such as generating responses to user queries, providing information, and performing tasks.

For example, you can use ChatGPT to generate responses for a customer service chatbot. When a user asks a question, the chatbot can use ChatGPT to generate a relevant and coherent response. You can also use ChatGPT to generate responses for a virtual assistant chatbot, such as answering questions, providing information, and performing tasks.

Virtual Assistants

Virtual assistants are computer programs that can simulate conversation with human users, similar to chatbots but with more advanced features and capabilities. Virtual assistants can be used in a wide range of applications, such as scheduling, reminder, and more.

ChatGPT can be used to generate text for virtual assistants, such as generating responses to user queries, providing information, and performing tasks. For example, you can use ChatGPT to generate responses for a virtual personal assistant, such as scheduling appointments, setting reminders, and providing information on weather, traffic, and news.

Language Translation

Language translation is the process of converting text from one language to another. ChatGPT can be used to generate text for language translation applications, such as translating text from one language to another.

For example, you can use ChatGPT to generate translations for a language translation application. When a user inputs text in one language, the application can use ChatGPT to generate a translation in another language.

Summarization

Text summarization is the process of creating a shortened version of a text. ChatGPT can be used to generate text for summarization applications, such as creating a summary of an article or news story.

For example, you can use ChatGPT to generate summaries for a news summarization application. When a user inputs a news article, the application can use ChatGPT to generate a summary of the main ideas of the article.

Creative Writing

ChatGPT can also be used in creative writing applications, such as writing poetry, composing music, and writing fiction. The model's ability to understand and generate human-like text, make it a powerful tool for creative writing.

For example, you can use ChatGPT to generate poetry, by providing a prompt and adjusting the temperature value to generate creative and unique text. You can also use ChatGPT to generate lyrics for a song, by providing a prompt and adjusting the top_p value to generate text that is more conservative or more creative.

In conclusion, ChatGPT can be used in a wide range of applications, from chatbots and virtual assistants to language translation and summarization, and even creative writing. By experimenting with different applications, you can discover new and exciting ways to use ChatGPT. Remember to fine-tune the model as needed and be aware of its potential biases and limitations. Have fun and be creative with the possibilities that ChatGPT offers!

7

Chapter 7: Managing and Scaling ChatGPT

In this chapter, we will explore the process of managing and scaling ChatGPT. As your use of ChatGPT grows, you may need to manage and scale the model to meet the demands of your application.

Managing the Model

Managing the model involves monitoring the performance of the model, fine-tuning it as needed, and keeping it updated. Here are some tips for managing the model:

1. Monitor the performance of the model: Keep track of the performance of the model by monitoring the quality and relevance of the output it generates. Make note of any issues or errors and fine-tune the model as needed.
2. Fine-tune the model: As the model is used, it may need to be fine-tuned to improve its performance. This can be done by training the model on a new dataset or by adjusting its parameters.
3. Keep the model updated: OpenAI releases updates to the model regularly. It's important to keep the model updated to ensure that it continues to perform well.

Scaling the Model

Scaling the model involves increasing the resources available to the model to handle an increase in demand. Here are some tips for scaling the model:

1. Increase the number of requests: As the demand for the model increases, you may need to increase the number of requests that the model can handle. This can be done by increasing the number of instances of the model or by using a more powerful machine.

Optimize the code: Optimizing the code can help to reduce the resources required by the model and increase its performance. This can be done by reducing the number of loops, minimizing the number of function calls, and using more efficient algorithms.

1. Use a Cloud-based solution: If you're running the model on-premise, consider using a cloud-based solution such as AWS, GCP or Azure. These providers offer a range of services that allow you to scale your resources up or down as needed.
2. Use caching: Caching can help to reduce the number of requests made to the model and improve its performance. For example, you can cache the output generated by the model and reuse it for similar requests.
3. Use load balancing: Load balancing can help to distribute the load across multiple instances of the model, improving its performance and availability.

Here's an example of how to scale ChatGPT using the OpenAI API:

```python
import openai

openai.api_key = os.environ.get("OPENAI_API_KEY")

# Increasing the number of requests
response = openai.Completion.create(
    model="text-davinci-002",
    prompt="Write a story about a robot that saves the world",
    max_tokens=1024,
```

```
    n = 4,
    stop=None
)


# Optimizing the code
# Use caching
# Use load balancing
```

In conclusion, managing and scaling ChatGPT is an important aspect of using the model in production. By monitoring the performance of the model, fine-tuning it as needed, and keeping it updated, you can ensure that the model continues to perform well. Scaling the model involves increasing the resources available to the model to handle an increase in demand, such as increasing the number of requests, optimizing the code, using caching and load balancing, and using cloud-based solutions.

It is important to remember that as you increase the resources, the cost will also increase. It's important to have a good understanding of the costs associated with running the model and to have a plan in place to manage them.

Another important aspect to consider when scaling the model is security. As the model is used to generate text, it is important to ensure that the data used to train the model is secure, and that the data generated by the model is protected.

Managing and scaling ChatGPT is a complex task that requires a good understanding of the model and the resources required to run it. By following the tips and guidelines outlined in this chapter, you can manage and scale ChatGPT to meet the demands of your application, while also ensuring the security and cost-effectiveness of the model.

8

Chapter 8: Advanced Topics

In this chapter, we will explore some advanced topics related to ChatGPT, such as controlling the temperature, handling large outputs, and working with multiple models.

Controlling the Temperature

Controlling the temperature is a technique that allows you to adjust the level of randomness in the output generated by ChatGPT. The temperature value ranges from 0 to 1, where a low temperature value (e.g. 0.1) generates conservative and predictable text, and a high temperature value (e.g. 0.9) generates creative and unpredictable text.

Here's an example of how to control the temperature when generating text with ChatGPT:

```python
import openai

openai.api_key = os.environ.get("OPENAI_API_KEY")

# Low temperature value (0.1)
response = openai.Completion.create(
    model="text-davinci-002",
    prompt="Write a story about a robot that saves the world",
    temperature=0.1
)
```

```python
# High temperature value (0.9)
response = openai.Completion.create(
    model="text-davinci-002",
    prompt="Write a story about a robot that saves the world",
    temperature=0.9
)
```

Handling Large Outputs

ChatGPT can generate large outputs, which can be difficult to handle and process. To handle large outputs, you can use the max_tokens parameter, which limits the number of tokens generated by the model.

Here's an example of how to handle large outputs with ChatGPT:

```python
import openai

openai.api_key = os.environ.get("OPENAI_API_KEY")

# Limiting the number of tokens generated
response = openai.Completion.create(
    model="text-davinci-002",
    prompt="Write a story about a robot that saves the world",
    max_tokens=1024
)
```

Working with Multiple Models

You can also work with multiple models in parallel, by creating multiple instances of the model and using them simultaneously. This allows you to generate text from different models and compare the results.

Here's an example of how to work with multiple models:

```python
import openai

openai.api_key = os.environ.get("OPENAI_API_KEY")

# Creating multiple instances of the model
```

```python
response1 = openai.Model.create(
    model="text-davinci-002",
    prompt="Write a story about a robot that saves the world"
)

response2 = openai.Model.create(
    model="text-curie-001",
    prompt="Write a story about a robot that saves the world"
)

# Using the models in parallel
response1 = openai.Completion.create(
    model=response1["id"],
    prompt="Write a story about a robot that saves the world"
)

response2 = openai.Completion.create(
    model=response2["id"],
    prompt="Write a story about a robot that saves the world"
)
```

In conclusion, controlling the temperature, handling large outputs, and working with multiple models are advanced techniques that can help you get more out of ChatGPT. By experimenting with different temperature values, you can generate text that is more conservative or more creative. By limiting the number of tokens generated by the model, you can handle large outputs more easily. And by working with multiple models in parallel, you can compare the results generated by different models. Remember to fine-tune the model as needed and be aware of its potential biases and limitations. Have fun and keep experimenting with the possibilities of ChatGPT.

9

Chapter 9: Conclusion

In this guide, we have covered the basics of using ChatGPT, a powerful language model developed by OpenAI. We have discussed its capabilities and limitations, and provided step-by-step instructions for implementing it in your applications.

We started by showing you how to register for an API key at OpenAI and how to use ChatGPT via the web browser, as well as how to use the command prompt. We also went into detail on how to setup ChatGPT, how to input and output text, and how to fine-tune the model to improve its performance.

We also explored the various applications of ChatGPT, including chatbots, virtual assistants, language translation, summarization, and creative writing. We also covered the important aspects of managing and scaling the model, and advanced topics such as controlling the temperature, handling large outputs, and working with multiple models.

It's important to remember that ChatGPT is a powerful tool that can generate human-like text, but it is not without its limitations. The model is based on a dataset of text and thus it can be affected by the same biases present in the data it was trained on. It's important to be aware of these biases and to fine-tune the model as needed.

In conclusion, ChatGPT is a powerful tool that can be used to generate text for a wide range of applications. With its ability to generate human-like text, it has the potential to revolutionize the way we interact with computers. We hope that this guide has provided you with the knowledge and tools you need to get started with ChatGPT and to discover new and exciting ways to use it. Happy coding!

10

Chapter 10: FAQ

In this chapter, we will provide answers to some frequently asked questions about ChatGPT.

Q: What is ChatGPT? A: ChatGPT (Conversational Generative Pre-training Transformer) is a large language model developed by OpenAI. It is trained on a dataset of text and can generate human-like text, making it useful for a wide range of applications, such as chatbots, virtual assistants, language translation, and more.

Q: How do I get an API key for ChatGPT? A: You can get an API key for ChatGPT by registering at **https://openai.com**. Once you have registered, you will receive an API key that you can use to access the model through the OpenAI API.

Q: How can I fine-tune ChatGPT for my specific use case? A: You can fine-tune ChatGPT for your specific use case by training it on a dataset that is relevant to your application. You can also adjust the parameters of the model, such as the temperature, to improve its performance.

Q: Can I use ChatGPT offline? A: Yes, you can use ChatGPT offline by using the OpenAI GPT-3 library, which allows you to download the model and use it in your local environment. However, you will need a powerful machine with a good GPU to run the model.

Q: Can ChatGPT handle multiple languages? A: Yes, ChatGPT can handle multiple languages, but it is trained primarily on English text. You can fine-tune the model on a dataset of text in another language to improve its performance.

Q: How can I avoid biases in the output generated by ChatGPT? A: You can avoid biases in the output generated by ChatGPT by fine-tuning the model on a diverse dataset and by being aware of the potential biases present in the data it was trained on. You can also evaluate the output generated by the model and adjust it as needed.

Q: Is there a limit on the number of requests I can make to the model? A: Yes, there is a limit on the number of requests you can make to the model, depending on your API plan. You can check your usage and limits in the OpenAI API dashboard.

Q: Can I generate outputs in different formats like images, audio etc? A: ChatGPT is primarily a text generation model and is not capable of generating outputs in formats such as images or audio. However, you can use other models or tools to convert the generated text into different formats.

Q: Can I generate outputs in different styles? A: Yes, you can generate outputs in different styles by fine-tuning the model on a dataset of text in the desired style and by adjusting the temperature and other parameters.

Q: Are there any limitations to the amount of text ChatGPT can generate? A: The amount of text ChatGPT can generate is limited by the available resources and the computational power of the machine it's running on. The model can generate large outputs, but there may be a tradeoff in terms of the quality and relevance of the generated text.

Q: Can I use ChatGPT in a commercial setting? A: Yes, you can use ChatGPT in a commercial setting, but you will need a paid API plan and you may need to comply with additional terms and conditions as set out by OpenAI.

Q: Can I get support or help if I have issues with ChatGPT? A: Yes, OpenAI provides support and help for issues related to ChatGPT through their website and community forum. You can also seek help from the developer community.

This concludes our chapter on frequently asked questions about ChatGPT. If you have any further questions or concerns, please refer to the OpenAI documentation or reach out to the OpenAI support team (https://help.openai. com/en/) for more information.

www.ingramcontent.com/pod-product-compliance
Lightning Source LLC
Chambersburg PA
CBHW071245140726
47996CB00007B/2763